KNIT TOGETHER IN LOVE

KNIT TOGETHER IN LOVE

A Focus for LDS Women in the 1990s

Carol L. Clark
Mary Ellen Edmunds
Anne C. Pingree
Cherry B. Silver

Deseret Book Company
Salt Lake City, Utah

Library of Congress Cataloging-in-Publication Data

Knit together in love : a focus for LDS women in the 1990s.
     p.   cm.
   Includes index.
   ISBN 0-87579-548-X
   1. Relief Society (Church of Jesus Christ of Latter-day Saints)
2. Women, Mormon.
BX8643.W4K65   1991
267′.449332 — dc20   91-27066
                                                             CIP

Printed in the United States of America

10   9   8   7   6   5   4   3   2

To the women of Relief Society —
our sisters, our friends

Contents

Preface

ix

Build a Personal Testimony
Cherry B. Silver

1

Bless the Individual Woman
Cherry B. Silver

17

Develop and Exercise Charity
Mary Ellen Edmunds

33

Strengthen Families
Anne C. Pingree

53

Enjoy a Unified Sisterhood
Carol L. Clark

69

Index

87

Preface

In our Relief Society sisterhood, everyone counts. Each woman matters. The mission of Relief Society reflects our desire that each of our sisters feels her eternal value as she enjoys the fruits of full gospel living.

The Mission of Relief Society

Build Personal Testimony (First Article of Faith)

Each woman is a daughter of God. She uses her agency to build her testimony and the testimonies of her family and others by being a thoughtful disciple, a student of the scriptures, and a prayerful, spiritual witness of the gospel of Jesus Christ.

Bless the Individual Woman (D&C 18:10)

Each woman lives righteously and joyfully as she stays true to her covenants with the Lord, shares in the blessings of the priesthood, values the diversity of others, and uses her abilities to extend, exemplify and teach.

Develop and Exercise Charity (Moroni 7:47)

Because "charity never faileth," charity is the keystone of Relief Society's mission statement. Each woman rejoices in truth as she develops and exercises qualities of charity in all aspects of her life.

Strengthen Families (D&C 88:119)

Each woman in each circumstance makes a home. She creates unity there and bases her home upon love of the Lord and love of each family member.

Enjoy a Unified Sisterhood (Mosiah 18:21–22)

As part of a sisterhood of righteous women, each woman shares faith, values, experience, ideas, friendship and love with her Relief Society sisters of all ages and circumstances.

In this book, members of the Relief Society General Board share their faith and insights about our wonderful worldwide Relief Society sisterhood and the mission that moves our work forward. We invite you to add your own perceptions to theirs as you share the mission of Relief Society with your sisters everywhere.

Sincerely,
Elaine L. Jack, President
Chieko N. Okazaki, First Counselor
Aileen H. Clyde, Second Counselor

Build a Personal Testimony

by Cherry B. Silver

Testimony does not come to us ready-made like a pre-fabricated house. A personal testimony represents a long-term construction project in which we are the master builders gathering our supplies and managing our tools. We are continually in process of erecting or strengthening testimony. Storms come that knock down sections of our house. We may be flattened by the fall. But with hope in Christ, we rise to rebuild it, perhaps more magnificently than before. "Build ye more stately mansions, O my soul," said the poet. ("The Chambered Nautilus," Oliver Wendell Holmes.)

Our building materials include our own actions and thoughts, our studies, our journal entries recording personal wrestling with life situations, our capacity for faith and hope. Our tools consist of prayer, scripture study, and thoughtful living as disciples of Christ. Experiences in the Church provide mortar. The resulting structure, if we have built on Christ, is stout with a door open through which we invite others to enter as we share our spiritual witness: "We believe in God, the Eternal Father, and in His Son, Jesus Christ, and in the Holy Ghost."

Faith. Faith is much like a muscle of the body. It grows in strength with activity and stretching. Paul taught that we possess a spiritual as well as a temporal nature. With the exercise of faith, gradually we mature spiritually until we learn to live in the light.

One reason to have study classes within the Church is to grow spiritually among sympathetic friends, sharing insights from our experiences and adding grace to grace as the Savior did.

As we mature in spirit, we begin to *act* on the measure of faith we now have. Faith, which "is not to have a perfect knowledge of things" (Alma 32:21), leads us to live by godly principles. And these nurturing actions help the plant to grow further. Test to see if it is good, counseled Alma, then share your results with others. Let your light shine. Be the salt with savor, be the leaven in the lump, taught Jesus Christ. (See Matthew 6.)

The image of leaven or yeast suggests expansion. People with the light of Christ carry the demeanor and have the words to change the feelings of people around them. Those who are "full of faith" begin to stir up goodness and spiritual forces that influence the circle of people around them and may expand to leaven their whole community.

When problems arise, neighbors turn to the friend

2

who radiates faith for her comfort and insights. "We can solve that," one Relief Society president in a little Hawaiian village used to say. She would open her arms to give a warm hug, offer a bowl of *saimin* to the visitor, then sit down to listen to troubles and pray together for understanding and relief.

Having faith to keep the commandments allows testimony to grow. A seamstress and mother of two children, as well as wife of a branch president in Abidjan, Cote d'Ivoire, bore her testimony based on life experiences as she taught Relief Society and made visiting teaching calls. "My husband couldn't get work for over a year. I made a little at my tailoring shop. Because we pay tithing and serve in the Church, other blessings come. Our family doesn't have as much sickness. We are able to shop wisely. And at the end of the month, although our money is gone, for some reason there is enough and we are still able to eat." The family was living with nonmember relatives through this period of unemployment. They could see their faith as the couple gathered their family for prayers in their room, studied gospel principles, took the bus long miles to church meetings, and made many sacrifices to keep their faith active.

There are many among us who, having once been touched by the message of the gospel, now lack faith and hope. What is the chance that these women can build a personal testimony anew?

One convert woman in Washington says, "I have so many questions. I need someone to listen to me, not to moralize, but to help me think these things through. We had wonderful home teachers who would come and talk with my husband and me, even two hours at a time. But we moved and haven't found that bond with anyone yet in our new town and new ward." Could friends from Relief Society provide that support? Can we nurture seeds of faith in one another?

A young adult woman in Utah who lives on her own and runs her own business talks of her emerging testimony: "My mother wants me to be a good church member. She set an example for me at home. But I needed to be independent and discover the truth for myself. Now that I have lived away from home for a while, I can see more clearly. I feel that I believe. Someday I'll come back." She needs models to follow and gentle encouragement from love.

Jesus gave straightforward advice to "try it" when He counseled, "My doctrine is not mine, but his that sent me. If any man will do his will, he shall know of the doctrine, whether it be of God, or whether I speak of myself." (John 7:16–17.)

To testify that moral living brings positive results, to say with certainty that commitment and sacrifice and paying tithing yield blessings, to witness that prayers are answered—all these testimonies come when we exercise our faith to live these principles and find that they come of God.

Hope. Hope is associated with the future. Particularly is it associated with our eternal future—through the redemption of Christ: "And what is it that ye shall hope for? Behold I say unto you that ye shall have hope through the atonement of Christ and the power of his resurrection, to be raised unto life eternal, and this because of your faith in him according to the promise." (Moroni 7:41.)

Hope sweetens life here, because hope opens spiritual windows. In October 1990 a Hungarian woman visited Salt Lake City to receive her endowment in the temple and obtain a patriarchal blessing. The blessing from the patriarch touched Ilona's heart. "He talked as if he knew all about me," she said. "There was a particular question in my life that I had confided only to my parents in Budapest, never to anyone here in the United States. Yet in the patriarchal blessing came an answer to that question. I know the Patriarch was speaking with understanding beyond his own. Another question of mine, he answered too, saying, 'That will come in the due time of the Lord.' What a relief I feel from the burdens I was carrying! I can act in the present. I can hope for the future."

Reading of some of our foremothers' lives reminds us that faith and hope made survival possible in the mud flats of Iowa in the winter of 1846–1847. Not only did women nurse others to ease the plaintive cries of the sick. Not only did families share their sacks of flour. But women living in wagon boxes or log huts gathered to sing and pray and bear spiritual witness together. And from the manifestations that followed, these women took hope. Yes, they worked diligently alongside their menfolk to improve health and housing for their frontier communities; but their goal was not a life of material ease. Many of them could have returned to comfortable conditions if they had renounced their faith and their gathering to Zion. These women lived according to a heavenly vision.

In our time, we too share the belief that we must help improve life conditions by working with other men and women to aid those unfairly treated by adverse social conditions, those burdened by poverty and illiteracy and injustice. We have an even grander hope. The woman of faith sees the panorama that reaches from birth to resurrection. When our mental windows are open to this vision of God's purposes, we cannot mourn that life right now is not fair. Instead, we act with hope that we can make a difference.

Thoughtful Discipleship. The "disciple" is a practitioner of the two great commandments — love of God, love of neighbor.

"If any man among you seem to be religious, and bridleth not his tongue, but deceiveth his own heart, this man's religion is vain.

"Pure religion and undefiled before God and the Father is this, To visit the fatherless and widows in their affliction, and to keep himself unspotted from the world." (James 1:26–27.)

"He hath shewed thee, O man, what is good; and what doth the Lord require of thee, but to do justly, and to love mercy, and to walk humbly with thy God?" (Micah 6:8.)

For thousands of years, prophets in the Judeo-Christian tradition have defined the essence of discipleship as consisting of acts of service and personal discipline.

Do our faces show that we are happy to be alive and doing? Can we radiate goodness and empathy with our eyes and smiles? Can we speak cordially to the store clerk, drive our cars with Christian charity, earnestly listen to the ideas of others and respond with kindly, encouraging words? No one is happy all of the time, but can we make the best of even negative situations, and let the light of Christ radiate through us?

When the government of Ghana padlocked the doors of the LDS chapels in June 1989 and ordered the missionary program shut down and all foreigners connected with the Church expelled, the news struck thousands of Ghanian members like a shock wave. No longer could they meet together in their buildings, or talk with their neighbors about the gospel, or partake of the ordinances together.

What could they do with their religious faith? Emma, the Ghanian Relief Society president in Nsawam, said, "I do miss the Church. I never knew how important church meetings are until the opportunity was taken away. . . . For the first two weeks I felt like someone whose dearly beloved one has been taken away suddenly. . . . Then my head began to ache and I became so tired I couldn't seem to get out of my room. So I took

7

the Book of Mormon and read the book of Alma. I keep reading till I feel better again. . . . I read some Church history. I think we the Ghanian Saints need the pioneer spirit. . . . I keep visiting the active sisters and they are all in good spirit. . . . I have tried to fast and pray more and better than I have ever done in all my life. My faith has increased greatly. . . . I used to be impatient in waiting; but now I know that God's time is the best. This stoppage has helped some of us to grow stronger in the gospel."

Emma is a thoughtful disciple of Christ who knew how to take the blessings of the gospel and Relief Society into the lives of others, even when the closed doors of the meetinghouses were guarded by soldiers and their faith was threatened. In December 1990, Ghanian Latter-day Saints were allowed to resume full church functions in their buildings.

Knowledge of Scriptures. Nephi taught a clear and simple doctrine when he said, "Ye shall press forward, feasting upon the word of Christ." (2 Nephi 31:20.)

Scriptures, keys to heavenly power, may unlock spiritual doors for us. In them daily messages from deity await us. We desire to *possess*, not simply *process*, the word of Christ.

One mother raised her children by the Psalms. They were her words of praise and of rebuke, her source of philosophy when problems arose. To be a practical student of the scriptures means that a woman loves and uses the writings of the prophets. It may not mean she knows everything "chapter and verse." But she *understands* and *uses* the messages of the scriptures. She retells the parables and stories to illustrate her lessons. She makes decisions by the wise words she finds there.

Loving the scriptures and reading in them regularly allows the Lord to send us daily messages. Elder Paul H. Dunn formed this provocative epigram: "When I want to talk to God, I pray. When I want God to talk to me, I read the scriptures."

A single woman, who is a convert to the Church, advises reading scriptures prayerfully with a pencil and notebook nearby. "What do I need to guide my life today?" she asks. In the middle of reading and pondering a chapter in the Bible, for instance, she feels particularly attracted to a verse or two. She writes these down and adds her thoughts or feelings or a way to apply these verses to herself. These personalized devotionals have sustained her through stormy seasons of life.

We are all in process of learning better how to use the scriptures. We can learn to feel the personality of the writers, to apply their teachings to life situations, and to seek the inspiration of the Lord for ourselves in these writings. Imbedded in these chapters are clues to divine principles as well as stories to warn and comfort, to chasten and inspire.

In the hunt for truth—amid arguments that everything is relative—the woman who understands scriptural messages holds an important key. She can choose enduring principles on which to base her behavior and guide others.

When a challenging assignment comes—whether serving a mission for eighteen months or teaching the nursery class for three weeks—we may think of Nephi's resolve: "I will go and do the things which the Lord hath commanded, for I know that the Lord giveth no commandments unto the children of men, save he shall prepare a way for them that they may accomplish the thing which he commandeth them." (1 Nephi 3:7.)

Nonbelievers may scoff at us for paying tithing, honoring the Sabbath day, or attending temple sessions, because the reasons and rewards for these practices relate to eternal rather than earthly logic. However, as we test these principles for ourselves, we find that they bless our lives in accordance with the Savior's advice: "If any man will do his will, he shall *know* of the doctrine, whether it be of God." (John 7:17.)

Prayer. Prayer has several purposes. For one thing, it may be a safeguard for us. We can ask for a mantle of protection to rest upon us so that, as we are tempted and tested by life experiences, we are ready with inspired choices. "Ye must watch and pray always lest ye enter into temptation" (3 Nephi 18:18), said the resurrected Savior, counseling us that we have an ever-present power available to us to resist negative thoughts and influences.

Another kind of prayer focuses on blessing others.

When a friend is sick or in trouble, we will pray for her or him, concentrating on the need.

Elder and Sister Marvin Bowden, as the Church's representatives in Kenya in 1988, were frequently stopped by the police and taken for questioning about our religious practices. Sometimes church meetings were interrupted and members threatened. During one interrogation, Sister Elva Bowden sat in an outer room, praying continually in her heart. Expulsion from the country, even imprisonment, could have been the outcome. As she prayed silently outside, antagonism decreased inside the room. Elder Bowden was able to explain principles from the missionary discussions to the police officers and lead them from threats to quiet listening. Finally, they released him.

Everyday needs are great. The Lord invites us to pray over our flocks and fields and to ask for our daily bread.

The Lord promises answers to our prayers, regardless of where we live or who we are, when we ask what is right. "And whatsoever ye shall ask the Father in my name, which is right, believing that ye shall receive, behold it shall be given unto you." (3 Nephi 18:20.)

One twenty-one-year-old woman described how she learned to pray effectively. "I was a college student wondering if I should finish school or go on a mission. I kept praying for God to make this decision for me. The answer didn't come, and I was confused and even angry. Then a friend made some suggestions on *how* to pray. When I was living as I best knew how, I invited the Spirit to guide me; then *I* made a decision and presented it to the

Lord, and I was flooded with a sense of rightness." In this manner confirmation came. She accepted a call to serve a mission in Argentina, where she faces more situations that require prayer and answers through the Spirit.

Covenants and Ordinances. A beautiful part of the spiritual world open to women is the making of covenants with God and the participating in ordinances that lead us back to our Heavenly Father. Reminders of these came as Moses organized the camp of Israel in the Sinai desert, as Brigham Young directed latter-day Israel for the crossing of the great plains, and, most supremely, as the Savior passed the cup for the Last Supper:

"Now therefore, if ye will obey my voice indeed, and keep my covenant, then ye shall be a peculiar treasure unto me above all people: for all the earth is mine." (Exodus 19:5.)

"And this shall be our covenant—that we will walk in all the ordinances of the Lord." (D&C 136:4.)

"Drink ye all of it; For this is my blood of the new testament, which is shed for many for the remission of sins." (Matthew 26:27–28.)

Ordinances are simple acts that bind and remind us. I was spiritually touched when an African husband baptized his wife in a quiet lagoon near Grand Bassam, Cote d'Ivoire, Africa, on April 25, 1988—the first baptism of a woman in that country. I sat with a congregation in Berlin after the wall was erected in the early 1960s, many of them elderly refugees from East Germany, as they partook of the bread and water of the sacrament and testified with bitter tears of their family losses and their need for Christ's solace. I know of an anxious husband and home teacher laying hands on the bandaged heads of wife and daughter, struck by a car, asking for life and recovery by the power they represented, according to their faith and God's will. And, after an all-night drive across three states, I was excited to enter the Provo temple with Mexican-American ward members where parents and grandparents received their endowments and three generations of a faithful convert family were sealed together in the new and everlasting covenant.

Personal testimonies are strengthened by acts of obedience in making sacred alliances with God. Because of these commitments, we are fortified to do his work.

Spiritual Witness. Alma taught that those desirous of coming into the fold of God would "stand as witnesses of God at all times and in all things, and in all places that ye may be in, even until death." (Mosiah 18:9.) At baptism we accept a commitment to proclaim God and bear witness of truth. Millions of Latter-day Saints, from Ireland to India, are living today as members of a religious minority among critical or even hostile peoples. It takes courage to bear witness.

The nearly fifty thousand full-time Latter-day Saint missionaries presently in 128 countries and territories of the world form an army of witnesses. Some of these have given their lives as part of their commitment. Others have sacrificed health. Most have experienced hardships and thereby have grown in their capacity to serve their

fellowmen empathetically, as Alma counseled his follow-
ers to do when they accepted the ordinance of baptism.
(See Mosiah 18:8–9.)

Parents of Elder Jeffrey Ball, who was one of two
American elders killed by terrorists in LaPaz, Bolivia, in
May 1989, have taken up his mission of love and testimony. A year after the shooting, they joined a human-
itarian expedition traveling from the United States to
Bolivia to bring medical aid and build greenhouses to
increase food supplies and reduce poverty among villagers
living in the *Altiplano*. Although Jeffrey had written in
his journal, "I am so content to be here," his mother
was afraid that she would be appalled by the conditions
she would find. She was concerned to know whether his
sacrifice had been worthwhile.

At a fireside in LaPaz, as the Balls met the Bolivians
their son had served, Sister Joyce Ball's concerns were
answered. "It was easy to see how he could feel so comfortable here," she said. "The Bolivian people became
examples to me, just the way they live. They lack material
things, but they have developed strong character." One
small man said he had prepared Jeff's body to come home.
Sister Ball could tell he had done so lovingly and that
Jeff had been just fine. "I am overwhelmed by how many
have been influenced by Jeff's sacrifice. We felt a broth-
erhood and sisterhood with them. When Christ comes,
I know many of them will be there."

Witness through Art. Great poetry and painting, music

14

and sculpture, and the creative use of textiles and stitchery, affirm the divine Creation and the Atonement.

Our Relief Society women are among those testifying of this light through their art. One example is the following poem, written for the Eliza R. Snow poetry contest by Mary Young, a young mother of eight children from Sumner, Washington. Her words dramatize the divine power of Christ, testified to by heavenly manifestations of light, linked to the birth, the mission, and the resurrection of the Son of God.

At the Garden Tomb, John 1:5

As a small sun arising out of turn,
Shines that great star in slow-wheeling night,
Rousing sheep and shepherds to angel hosannas
For cave-born Babe in a slumbering hill-town.

By the second hour the morning mists are burning,
And glinting off the Galilee dazzle the stony hillsides
Where the Words of light are flowing, flowing,
And only the sightless are seeing.

And here in an hour before the dawning comes
The rising of that Son in soul-burst dark-drenching
   wakening,
Day-breaking gathering of star and sun and Word,
All light coming full in a great and shining circle.

(*Ensign*, March 1986.)

These artists are motivated by a spirit outside themselves, which we can tap also as we desire to strengthen our witness of truth: "If you shall ask the Father in my

15

name, in faith believing, you shall receive the Holy Ghost, which giveth utterance, that you may stand as a witness of the things of which you shall both hear and see, and also that you may declare repentance unto this generation." (D&C 14:8.)

Relief Society sisters worldwide are builders through testimony — starting with a desire, nurturing faith, strengthening hope, working with scriptures and prayer, and living as thoughtful disciples, so that all become spiritual witnesses, giving utterance in words and action to the truths we live by through the power of the Holy Ghost.

Bless the Individual Woman

by Cherry B. Silver

"Remember the worth of souls is great in the sight of God." (D&C 18:10.)

We the 5.5 billion people of Planet Earth form an immensely colorful and diverse parade of faces. Our outward appearances differ from the stocky, kerchiefed women shoppers lined up before the meat shops of Warsaw, Poland, to the black-veiled Muslim wives of Cairo gliding to market with baskets in hand and the Bolivian women of the *Altiplano* hoeing potatoes in bowler hats and petticoats.

Chromosones and genes and DNA cells cluster in infinite variation to make each hand, each body build, each turn of the lips and shape of the eyes, each mind and memory different in every person. All people are endowed with individual personalities, individual ways of thinking, individual agency. This suits God's purposes and adds to His glory.

The Apostle Paul, who sailed the Mediterranean and trekked overland to bring the gospel of Christ to Jews and Gentiles of diverse backgrounds, sought an image to express the beauty and usefulness of all this diversity blended into one.

> For as the body is one, and hath many members, and all the members of that one body, being many, are one body: so also is Christ.
> But now hath God set the members every one of them in the body, as it hath pleased him.
> And if they were all one member, where were the body?
> And the eye cannot say unto the hand, I have no need of thee: nor again the head to the feet, I have no need of you. (1 Corinthians 12:12, 18, 19, 21.)

Not only is diversity healthy, it is necessary to make a functioning body. No part is unworthy. So, continued Paul, we are part of an essential unity. We function together. If one part suffers, so do we all. If one part is honored, the others rejoice.

In the history of mankind, caste systems and prejudice against ethnic groups and gender have created misery for many of God's children. Jesus confounded the orthodox leaders of His time because He refused to follow their prescribed formulae. He dined with publicans, He talked with Samaritans, He included instead of excluded all people — women, children, publicans, the lame, the diseased, the sinners.

As members of this worldwide organization called

Relief Society, our mission is clear. In all our diversity we combine our strengths to bless each other and to do the work of the Lord.

Relief Society blesses the lives of individual women to live joyfully and righteously.

As Latter-day Saint women, we blend our efforts to help each woman discover and develop her particular gifts, in order that we may all contribute to the "body of Christ."

In her conference open house address in September 1990, President Elaine Jack stated, "The Lord is concerned about every individual. And so are we in Relief Society." We welcome the diversity that exists among the 2.8 million women of Relief Society in the world. In diversity of ages and talents, viewpoints and cultures, lies strength.

Spiritual Witness. Each woman is important to the Lord and has the right to His blessings. Each has the right, first, to pray to God our Father. And each may receive a personal witness of the Christ.

When the resurrected Savior appeared to the people of the American continent, He invited them to feel the prints in His hands and feet, "that ye may know that I am the God of Israel, and the God of the whole earth, and have been slain for the sins of the world." He had the multitude come forward and one by one test for himself, "and this they did do, going forth one by one until they had all gone forth." (3 Nephi 11:14–15.)

Jesus did not judge that only the leaders should come forth, nor only the men, nor only the grown-ups. Nor did he separate one race from another. The brown-skinned and lighter-skinned believers listened together. He accepted all as worthy of individual testimony.

Personal Mission. A second right we have as children of God is guidance in fulfilling our individual missions in life.

What purpose does God have for us, each as an individual? That is a question worth asking. What does He want each of us to accomplish with the life He has given us?

"Trust in the Lord with all thine heart; and lean not unto thine own understanding. In all thy ways acknowledge him, and he shall direct thy paths." (Proverbs 3:5–6.)

A path is not a highway. The surface of a path might be irregular, and our feet inclined to trip on the bumpy surface as we find our way (see Jeremiah 18:15), so we need a guide.

The writers of scripture speak frequently of two paths: The wise father counsels his child to avoid the "path of the wicked," which "is as darkness" (Proverbs 4:14, 19), but respond to godly instruction, for the "path of the just is as the shining light" (Proverbs 4:18). Lehi's dream offered a rod of iron alongside the path, something to hold on to when the mists of darkness roll over the way and confuse us and when the taunts of the unbelievers make staying on the path unpopular.

Bless the Individual Woman

In 1976 our family—which consisted of me, my husband, and our two young children—were touring the bush country of Cote d'Ivoire, West Africa, by private car. The dirt road we were on narrowed in the grasses into not much more than a path. Then it became a raised causeway. We could see no sign of habitation. We speeded up, liking this grand highway taking us into the bush.

Unexpectedly, from out of the distance, a freight truck came lumbering toward us. We slowed after he passed us, surprised because he wasn't on our causeway, but on a lower make-shift road, running parallel to ours.

Why had he avoided our lofty, fast-traveling causeway? We slowed the speed of our car and moved forward cautiously to examine what lay before us. There came in the road a sheer drop-off of ten feet producing a fifteen-foot-wide gash. If we had continued at our original speed, our car would have plunged over the edge, nose first, and smashed. We could have been injured or killed; certainly we would have been stranded in the bush, far from any helping hands.

We were trembling, but felt blessed to have stopped. And we were struck by the sheer miracle of the truck having come when it did to warn us of the need to detour.

After we backed up to find a place to descend to the lower road on which the truck had come, we continued driving, but the marked path dwindled after a few kilometers more and finally ended in the grassy prairie, with no village nearby. We realized a greater miracle was involved than we had thought. There was no *earthly* reason why a freight truck should have been coming toward us. We believe, however, there was a *heavenly* reason why it came when we needed to change our path to prevent accident and perhaps even death.

This is a modern parable. Our own understanding is limited, and our resources are feeble. Two years ago I sat trapped in our car in Kinshasa, Zaire, pinned by a soldier sprawled across my lap. He, along with three others, was struggling with my husband in the driver's seat, trying to wrest the car keys from the ignition and push us off the road. Four other military men with rifles surrounded our vehicle. My husband kept possession of the keys. The soldier continued to demand control of our car and searched my purse and papers while the rest glowered at us. All the while I prayed silently, "We are trying to be your missionaries. Guide our words and actions. Soften their hearts." Finally the soldiers' superior officer responded to their radioed message for help, drove up, heard our story, and guided us back on our way. How reassuring it is to trust in Him and feel our paths directed!

I have made decisions in my life that have made me shake my head and wonder why I did what I did—such as the time I bought a bookstore. Looking back on three frustrating years of traveling down that track, I see that I gained experiences Heavenly Father was willing I should have. There were no business profits, but managing a business opened doors to participation in a local service organization alongside outstanding women of many religious faiths. That involvement could not have come any other way. I also started a free weekly class for writing family history in the mornings in the little store. During the day my husband and I often talked about religious beliefs with customers who came. We were able to be witnesses of truth and in a distinctive way bless others.

Strength in Bearing Burdens. In the Savior's atoning mission is the ultimate reason for bearing the burdens we do. Our faith in Him steadies our efforts and keeps our hopes bright. We feel His joy only after difficult decisions, hard labor, even suffering.

Anyone who has lived or traveled in developing areas of the world sees women supporting immense burdens. They know poverty and sickness and hopelessness. Women worry about finding adequate shelter, daily food, paid work for family members, education for their children.

In many areas, diseases such as malaria, polio, leprosy, tuberculosis, dysentery and dehydration, worms, and now AIDS lower life expectancy. High infant mortality rates occur. Malnutrition and poor sanitation affect every age group.

In parts of Africa, Asia, and South America, education is meager and unemployment rates run 30 to 70 percent. As a result, young men stand around on street corners and girls work for very low wages as domestics. The underuse of intelligence and energy represents a tragic loss of human resources.

Despite these huge problems, one also sees smiling

faces and surprisingly cheerful women at work, carrying water in buckets on their heads or trudging to market, with a baby strapped to the back.

In branches and wards of the Church worldwide, our women counsel together. They uplift each other by sharing spiritual experiences. They teach each other how to solve practical problems. We are resources to each other to bless our lives.

People working together effect change for good. A village cooperative of women makes bricks to improve their housing in Nigeria. Kenyans lay out an irrigation system for their crops. Bolivians, trying to farm despite a short growing season, learn to lay up adobe walls to make simple greenhouses, topped with heavy clear plastic. Mothers in the Philippines learn to mix rehydration solutions to prevent deaths from dysentery. Together we can make a difference.

Express Individual Creativity. A few years ago a woman college president in Massachusetts initiated a program for creative minds in science and the humanities in which women are supported in their research and writing. "An atmosphere of expectation," Mary Bunting, the college president, called the creating of an environment where women do their best. Here barriers are pushed aside and others wait to receive and profit from their efforts.

Relief Society itself is a kind of institute of higher education, providing a network of expectation and support. Every time we meet to study, create, extend ourselves to others, serve shoulder to shoulder, or visit in

each other's homes, we demonstrate an ongoing education program. Our immediate goal is to improve each
individual life here; our ultimate goal is to live joyously
with loved ones and our eternal parents forever.

As in the parable of the talents, each of us has gifts
to share with others. There are artistic talents, there are
gifts of courtesy and counsel, there are talents of perse-
verance and courage. The Lord expects us to search for
our personal gifts and let them shine through to bless
ourselves and others.

One multi-talented woman, now at retirement age,
has shared her talents all her life. Never married herself,
she has contributed to her extended family and, when
living away from them, has made Church members her
family. She has a rich contralto voice and has blessed
her community through her gift of song. She is also a
skilled social worker, and she still volunteers her time to
bishops, counseling with their members. In retirement
she is a temple ordinance worker. She has magnified her
gifts. And best of all, she lives with a spirit of sensitivity
to others, based on her own solid self-esteem. She radiates
spiritual health.

This gift of self-esteem grows as each of us recognizes
our individuality and accepts our differences from others.
A healthy sense of self-worth, says one commentator,
requires investing time and effort in ourselves. A woman
believing in herself first "takes charge of her own self-
development." Second, she decides to make a "growing,
life-long investment" in herself. Third, she gives herself

"the right to have opinions, beliefs, values and positions that are different from those of others — without penalty." Fourth, she knows she is "intrinsically valuable simply because she is" and that she can make errors without labeling herself as "dumb." Fifth, she develops "multiple sources for love and nurturance and stimulation," rather than relying on just one other person, whether parent or husband or friend. And sixth, she comes to understand herself by looking inward and by reading wisely in books and articles that help her develop "a firm sense of self." (JoAnn Larsen, "Make Developing Self an Objective in Your Life," *Deseret News,* November 11, 1990.)

Overcoming Obstacles. It sometimes takes courage to discover the best in ourselves and to improve our lot in life. A young woman graduate student in genetics at BYU was praised by her faculty adviser because she "is highly skilled with laboratory equipment, is meticulous in her research, and is a welcome help for the students she counsels."

Yet this young woman is nearly blind; devastated by her failing eyesight, she once dropped out of high school. "She found herself caught in societal attitudes that, she said, dictate a lesser status for those who are blind. 'Society has told blind people they are dependent and not normal, and I believed that for awhile,' she said. 'On my own and through help . . . I've come to realize it doesn't have to be that way.

" 'I've learned that my Heavenly Father loves me and I believe He knows me. I believe that I am physically

26

acceptable to Him; therefore, why shouldn't that be good enough for me? Blind people can function on an equal basis if given the proper training and opportunities. I'm normal; I just sometimes need different tools.' " (*Church News*, November 3, 1990.)

Multiply her example by hundreds and thousands of other women with disabilities, mental and physical and social, still finding a way to express the divine spirit within them. The mathematics of despair tell us that self-doubt feeds upon itself. When we depend on others to validate us, we are supersensitive to put-downs. Discouragement naturally follows. But this needn't be. As one observer asks, "Is what others think of us more important than what God thinks of us?"

Agency. An eternal gift shared by God with all His children is the power of choice. He expects us to use this power wisely and with courage.

> For behold, it is not meet that I should command in all things. . . .
> Verily I say, [women] should be anxiously engaged in a good cause, and do many things of their own free will, and bring to pass much righteousness;
> For the power is in them, wherein they are agents unto themselves. And inasmuch as [women] do good they shall in nowise lose their reward. (D&C 58:26–28.)

Because we are held responsible, women need to be concerned about their "weight." This does not refer to pounds around the hips. The kind of "weight" we need to focus on is the weight of our judgments, personality, and spirit.

Women have tremendous power to change the world around them for good. Some of that influence can be manifest in school parent-teacher organizations, in political districts and town councils, and in volunteer service projects. Certainly our attitudes and dispositions shape human lives within our immediate spheres of family life, work, and community.

At other times, women need to lean their weight on resolving social problems and moral issues. If crime and drugs, poverty and homelessness, inflict our cities, solutions may come from the common sense and well-chosen words and actions of good women.

Speaking out on political and social issues needs to follow hard thinking and solid research and mature deliberation. Thoughtful women can promote righteous principles with their best energies but without bigotry, all the while allowing others to exercise their own agency to choose.

President Spencer W. Kimball expressed great hope in the power of women to articulate principles of faith and be an influence in the world. "Much of the major growth that is coming to the Church in the last days will come because many of the good women of the world (in whom there is often such an inner sense of spirituality) will be drawn to the Church in large numbers. This will happen to the degree that the women of the Church reflect righteousness and articulateness in their lives and to the degree that they are seen as distinct and different — in happy ways — from the women of the world." (*My Beloved Sisters*, Deseret Book Company, Salt Lake City, 1980, p. 44.)

He describes the great blessing we women can be to others, as we demonstrate that our choices and distinctive life patterns work well in our multifaceted contemporary world.

One Church member defined "agency" more narrowly when she complained: "I don't want the Church telling me what to do. I have my free agency, don't I?" What this member is forgetting is her role as a child of God in a universe of eternal laws. She can accept or reject wise principles of living from an inspired source, but must take the consequences. We have a stewardship and we are held accountable.

When Lehi talked about freedom of choice, he specified the alternatives and showed the consequences: "Men [and women] . . . are free to choose liberty and eternal life, through the great Mediator of all men, or to choose captivity and death." (2 Nephi 2:27.)

Life presents difficult choices. We don't always pick our route. But we can choose our guide. Our basic choice of eternal values helps us manuever through the obstacles on our road.

Transitions. We may believe that we are walking a good path, and then destiny brings us to a fork in the road and we face uncertainties again. We call these "the transitions" of life. And the transitions that confront us are diverse. Shakespeare's Jacques (in *As You Like It,* Act II, Scene 7) recounts seven ages of man from infant to elder. We could probably add a few.

Who is in transition among us? The Young Adults are, as they move from adolescence to young womanhood. The elderly are, as they lose friends and have physical activity curtailed by declining health and mobility. There are those entering marriages and those leaving them, through widowhood or divorce. Some are adding children to their homes, others are seeing children leave, and still others are receiving back "the boomerang generation"— children who left once and are returning, sometimes with children of their own. Women are in transition when they make career changes or reach retirement for self or spouse.

All the transitions of life require special understanding and help. And Relief Society sisters can be there to bless each other in our individual needs.

Extend, Teach, Exemplify. Extending a hand of help is a natural gesture in every culture. When an African child dies, the mother's women friends gather in the home to wail with her around the corpse. Neighbors help prepare food to feed the circle of mourners. At the graveside, a prayer of dedication is said. Friends may leave gifts to help the family, but after the burial, life must resume its normal course. The wailing stops, the mother says, "So be it," and she takes up again her daily work.

Customs vary from culture to culture, but the desire to help each other is universal. Visualize the extending that goes on around you. Blessed by gospel insights and by the power of the priesthood, women have great powers for ministering to world needs. In Relief Society, the programs called visiting teaching and compassionate service mobilize us to exercise watchcare over each other. We see needs and try to meet them. We are learning to be guided by the Spirit in seeing and responding.

Relief Society women exemplify a wide range of godly life-styles. They act as civic leaders and volunteers at homeless shelters; they head service organizations; they write letters to their congressmen; they help in local schools; they plant gardens and rake their leaves. They search for the truth and teach truth by word and by example. They are contributors to life.

"Remember the worth of souls is great in the sight of God." (D&C 18:10.) Relief Society women worldwide are themselves blessed. And they bless others.

Develop and Exercise Charity

by Mary Ellen Edmunds

One day a friend and I were in the "Avenues" in Salt Lake City going somewhere, and we noticed a young mother looking very frustrated and unhappy standing out by her truck. We were prompted to stop, and did. She had run out of gas on her way to pick up a daughter from a dancing lesson, and she couldn't believe the bad luck. Several other children were with her, watching and waiting.

We said we'd get some gas for her; and while she seemed grateful for the help, there was also the awkwardness of being on the "receiving end." We drove until we found a gas station, got a couple of gallons in a container we borrowed from them, then returned and put the gas in the truck.

The woman was thankful but still seemed uncomfortable. Then an idea came and I said to her, "You'd do the same for us!" That stopped her. She thought about it, then broke into a smile. "You're right! I would!" And all of us would, wouldn't we . . . if we just *knew.* There are so many more ways that we *can know!* I can no longer remember where I was going that day, or what else happened. The thing I remember is the sweet experience of stopping and helping in a little way and making a big difference.

There was a new commandment which the Savior shared: "Love one another as I have loved you." Constantly, patiently, unconditionally, almost like: "Do unto others as they *want* you to do unto them, as they *need* you to do." As Christ prompts us to do. Many times, in many ways, our Heavenly Father gives us specific opportunities to develop and practice that kind of love, that depth of love. To share with each other, to serve each other, to develop more of the godliness that is within us. The mercy, the patience, the cheerfulness, the genuine kindness.

I suppose you can have service without love, but I don't think you can have genuine charity — pure love — without service. I don't think it's possible to feel compassion without being *compelled* to do something to help. Charity — the pure love of Christ — is the greatest force on this earth, and one of the *only* things powerful enough to change all the trouble in this world.

I remember hearing, as a young child, the phrase "charity never faileth." I knew it was somehow associated with Relief Society. And indeed it is — and has been since 1842. This motto was chosen in a different time and place, but is just as powerful now for us as it was for them then. Charity is at the heart of Relief Society. It is at the center of providing relief, and it is critical to building a society. With charity this can happen even though members of the society are miles and continents away from each other, with uniqueness in their daily activities and the demands on their days, hours, and energy. It is a gift we can cultivate and pray for—the ability to love everyone everywhere in a Christlike, tender way.

I think I know a *lot* more now about what charity means and why it never fails. I am deeply grateful to belong to an organization which has chosen "Charity Never Faileth" as a motto for each of its nearly 3 million members. I'm thankful that the whole program of Relief Society puts us in situations where we develop and ex-ercise charity—opportunities to visit and serve each other, to learn and share in a variety of settings that build sisterhood. To worship and mourn and rejoice and sing and meet together oft. To "be remembered and nourished by the good word of God, to keep [each other] in the right way, to keep them continually watchful unto prayer, relying alone upon the merits of Christ, who was the author and the finisher of their faith. And the church did meet together oft, to fast and to pray, and to speak one with another concerning the welfare of their souls." (Moroni 6:4–5.) Thank goodness for the gospel of Jesus Christ, His Church, and Relief Society!

We find examples of charity in the scriptures. Mor-mon teaches what charity means to him. He defines this pure love and points out that "if ye have not charity, ye are nothing, for charity never faileth. Wherefore, cleave unto charity, which is the greatest of all, for all things must fail—But charity is the pure love of Christ, and it endureth forever; and whoso is found possessed of it at the last day, it shall be well with him." (Moroni 7:46–47.) What a promise! What a declaration about the importance of this quality—this depth of love which helps us to *be* good and to *do* good!

I took some time to explore definitions for the words used in Moroni 7 and I Corinthians 13 to come to a better understanding of charity. What an instructive experience! I've gone through the list of qualities and characteristics, and thought carefully about each one.

Charity *suffereth long.* To suffer is to endure, bear, allow, permit, tolerate. Job suffered long. So did Christ. So have countless others.

Charity is *kind*—friendly, gentle, tenderhearted, and generous.

Charity *envieth not.* There is no discontent or ill will because of another's advantages, possessions, etc. No desire to get something that belongs to someone else.

Charity *vaunteth not itself.* One who has charity does not brag or boast or seek to be above another. Was Christ teaching us of charity when He said that "he that is greatest among you shall be your servant?" (Matthew 23:11.) Was He helping us know how to develop and exercise charity when He reminded us that being in the service of others was as if we had done it unto Him? (See

Mosiah 2:17–22; Matthew 25:40.) What about His message that every man should esteem His brother as himself (see D&C 38:24–27), and that we should remember in all things the poor and the needy? (See D&C 52:40.) In deed as well as in word, He pointed out that those who had should share with those who had not (Mosiah 18:26–28), and that those who were strong should help those who were weak (Romans 15:1). He asked that we feed His sheep — that we act towards others as He, the Good Shepherd, does and would.

When we're filled with charity we're *not puffed up.* We do not want praise unduly. It's exhausting to constantly put ourselves above another. This is sometimes called being a "Topper." Or a "Bottomer." Sometimes moms do that. Did you ever come home and say you'd had a hard day in junior high and have your mom say, "Well, when I was your age I had to rollerskate fifty miles to babysit for five cents an hour." That's a bottomer. What's a "topper"? Someone says to you, "My son got an A on a chemistry paper," and you respond with, "Well *my* son has been invited to open up a yogurt shop on the moon." That's a topper. Neither a "topper" nor a "bottomer" be. It's too big a drain on your battery. Rejoice in what *you* can do, as well as in what others can do. One person drags around her family history stuff: "I'm back to Noah!" And you respond with, "I'm back to my mother!"

Charity does not *behave itself unseemly.* We avoid that which is indecent or unbecoming.

Charity *seeketh not her own*. There are no "exclusive groups" — one possessed of this pure love reaches out to everyone everywhere. We can visit those who can't come to visit us. We can practice becoming better listeners. We can speak to people we don't know (yet) and be the first to be friendly and to get acquainted. We can work to have a countenance which shows love to everyone. There is much to be learned about charity through our own experiences — with sorrow as well as joy. We can spend time with children who can help us to be more childlike, more charitable. The same is true as we spend time with "senior saints" who many times feel neglected and forgotten.

Those who develop charity are *not easily provoked*. They are patient, and are not easily angered or irritated. The real Christian is not "touchy," and doesn't have a quick temper and is not impatient. Love is calm — not in a hurry; love takes time. We can't always "do what Jesus would do" for an hour and see dramatic results. Some of the changes you bring in your life and in the world will likely take two hours, or two years, or your whole life. The trees don't bear fruit the morning after you plant seedlings.

Those with charity *think no evil*. They are always looking for the good in people, situations, experiences. We need to forgive each other. Christ did — and what if one stood near who with great horror realized what he had done, and then heard those tender words from a dying God: "Father, forgive them . . . they don't know

what they're doing." Maybe we should forgive each other, ·
because we don't know what we're doing, either. We *all*
make mistakes. We're all trying.

Charity causes us to *rejoice not in iniquity*, or inequity.
We do not desire to put ourselves above or below anyone.
We also work to avoid inequity between what we know
we want to be doing and what we are actually doing. We
want to have harmony and inner peace.

Charity *rejoiceth in the truth* — in that which is established as fact, as principle. Those with charity strive to
be true: sincere, genuine, honest; and in agreement with
established standards.

Charity *beareth all things*. To bear means to undergo
successfully; capable of withstanding; to permit; to sustain
the burden of, perhaps including the lightening of others'
burdens.

Charity *believeth all things*, having confidence in a
statement or promise of another person, especially God.
Hopeth all things — a desire accompanied by anticipation;
trust; reliance. *Endureth all things* — to last, continue, remain; to bear.

And then, *charity never faileth:* it never lacks, falls
short; never deceives or disappoints; is never insufficient;
never loses strength or power; is never negligent; never
weakens; is never useless or unhelpful; never abandons;
never leaves, omits, or neglects. No wonder! After going
carefully through these words and characteristics, no
wonder this pure love never fails!

I've met people who are examples of this pure love

of Christ. They include my parents, friends, and loved ones in different lands. They've been my teachers and have shown me why charity doesn't fail. What a marvelous thing—that we have something in our lives that will *never fail,* to have something which will endure forever! So much in life *does* fail—our brakes, our teeth, our phone, our furnace, even our hearts and some relationships. Food spoils and treasures break and batteries wear out and something that was a great invention a few years ago has been replaced with something fancier, faster, and finer. But love—charity—never faileth. It is constant and powerful.

Pure love and service with compassion often requires sacrifice. At the very least, inconvenience. People seldom begin a sweet story of an extraordinary experience of helping or serving (exercising charity) with, "It was on a day and at a time when I didn't have anything at all to do and I was just about to call everyone I know to see if they wanted me to do something." Usually it starts, "I was so busy that day. I had so much on my mind, and so much on my list of things to do. I had a headache, the basement had just flooded, my baby had swallowed a roll of film. . . . " The Good Samaritan was on his way to a prayer meeting.

Someone might ask, "Can you help me?" and if it wouldn't be too much trouble I cheerfully respond, "Sure. I don't have anything else to do." But what if I *do* have something else to do? Something important. Do I trust God enough to know He'll not give me a commandment (a prompting, an opportunity to serve, a feeling to reach out) without helping me to accomplish it? So many times when I've been late for something or have missed something I felt was important, it has turned out to be for a good reason. Maybe someone needed something, and I was in a position to help. I find I need to more often "be still and know."

Have you ever thought that someone somewhere may be pleading with Heavenly Father for help, and *you* may be the one chosen to help answer that prayer? If we're willing, He'll use us. You likely have no idea how often you *rescue* someone. "Who *is* that?" someone will say as you pass by. "Why did I feel so much love?" Maybe it's your countenance, the love that they see in your eyes. They come close to you and feel so safe. You provide a refuge. As you think of your life, of the times that stand out and you have really lived, it's usually when you've done things in the spirit of love. Not necessarily "*big*" things. Lots of times it's the *little* things.

Love takes a lot of energy. A lot of work. And remember, sometimes we *can* help, and sometimes we *can't*. We do the best we can do, and some days are better than others. Everyone does what he can, according to what he hath—according to the extent of his ability.

How do we develop charity? It doesn't just "happen" after a certain number of years go by. We are commanded to pray for this gift. What are you willing to do? That's where we start—we are *willing*. Willing to bear one another's burdens, willing to mourn with them, comfort them, take upon us His name — be Christians. Christlike. Covenant people. When we are willing to do loving, kind things, ideas come as to when, and who, and why and how. Where there's a *will* there's a *way*. And Christ has said, "I am the way," and we follow His example. He needs our help to show others the way, the way to come unto Him.

There are many ways we can develop and recognize charity in ourselves and others. We can consciously do things which bring more compassion and gentleness into our hearts and our actions. Charity is not only the "act," the "doing," but that which compels us to act and to do — the tender, compassionate feelings in our souls which won't let us ignore someone who needs us. Charity is a condition of the heart, and a conditioning of the heart.

We can develop charity by seeking promptings to contact someone who is in need. We can actually exercise this capacity to be responsive to the Spirit and to become a more effective instrument in God's hands. Think of someone *specific* whom you need to telephone or write or visit. Make a plan to do so. We can work to cheerfully and willingly respond to opportunities for service even when it's inconvenient. We can respond to those who have a need to *give* by accepting their help and kindness with gratitude and joy.

How about some "Low Tech Love," for those who don't have a lot of extra time, energy, money, food, ideas, clothing, whatever. Try "low-tech" love. These are things "anyone" can do. Even busy, busy, busy worldlings.

Don't wait for the *big deal*. Just serve here and now. Love is a lot of "little" rescues and burdens lifted and people genuinely served. Be kind to those right around you, close to you — otherwise your help, your compassion and kindness, may be *imaginary:* "If I were there . . . " Or the "when/then" trap. "When" never comes, so neither does "then."

Have you ever sat in a busy place such as an airport or a shopping mall and watched people — their faces, their nonverbal messages, their interaction with others? It seems to bring compassionate feelings as you try to imagine what their challenges and burdens might be. Charity is cooperation, teamwork, unselfish sharing of responsibilities *and* the "spotlight." It is love at home and kind words to each other. A woman who is a successful attorney said, "Charity just means that people love each other. And if people did love each other the way they should, it might not be good for my practice, but it would be good for the world."

Give love to those who can't return it right now. Give compliments. Find one. Even if it's hard some days. "Uh, son. I . . . uh . . . like the way you breathe. Yes! It's wonderful the way you breathe in and out, in and out, all the time. Faithfully. You're such a faithful son. So dependable in your breathing!"

Here's a motto to try: *"Wait a week."* Wait a week, and then give praise for something. It may mean even more to someone to know you still remember a whole week later. "I want to thank you for what you shared in

43

your talk about families (your lesson on faith, your comment in class on commitment). I've been thinking about it this past week and it has meant so much to me. You're in my journal!" What might that mean to someone?

Notice those you haven't been noticing. How about the deacons in your ward. What would it mean to them and do to them if *you* noticed them. Let's talk to the deacons, the Sunbeams, the Mia Maids, and the senior Saints. Select someone with whom you've been having a hard time, and go to them and "make up." A sister-in-law, a neighbor, whoever. They'll be so surprised. So happy. So thankful. Say something like, "I set a goal not to talk to you for a whole year. I've now reached that goal, and I'm tired of being miserable. Can we talk?" Or, "I've been appointed chairman of the Neighborhood Ash Wednesday celebration, and we wonder if you could please donate a pickle and two paper plates?" Have you noticed that it's hard for someone to close their door *or* their heart when someone approaches them with pure love?

Charity is developed as we try to more fully live the law of the fast. This important law of God is more than going without food and paying a minimum amount for meals missed. It seems tied to responding to those who are hungry, thirsty, and experiencing other needs. And, oh, the promises! As we reach out to others, we will always find God is there.

> Is not this the fast that I have chosen? to loose
> the bands of wickedness, to undo the heavy burdens,

and to let the oppressed go free, and that ye break every yoke?

Is it not to deal thy bread to the hungry, and that thou bring the poor that are cast out to thy house? when thou seest the naked, that thou cover him; and that thou hide not thyself from thine own flesh?

Then shall thy light break forth as the morning, and thine health shall spring forth speedily: and thy righteousness shall go before thee; the glory of the Lord shall be thy rereward.

Then shalt thou call, and the Lord shall answer; thou shalt cry, and he shall say, Here I am. If thou take away from the midst of thee the yoke, the putting forth of the finger, and speaking vanity;

And if thou draw out thy soul to the hungry, and satisfy the afflicted soul; then shall thy light rise in obscurity, and thy darkness be as the noonday;

And the Lord shall guide thee continually, and satisfy thy soul in drought, and make fat thy bones; and thou shalt be like a watered garden, and like a spring of water, whose waters fail not.

And they that shall be of thee shall build the old waste places: thou shalt raise up the foundations of many generations; and thou shalt be called, The repairer of the breach, The restorer of paths to dwell in. (Isaiah 58:6–12.)

The deeper our relationship with God, the more we will long to serve and love Him, and to make ourselves ready for anything He needs us to do. As we come unto Christ we can turn and help others do the same, which is the mission and purpose of the Church and gospel. The scriptures are the "handbook" of instructions for those who wish to love and serve the way the Savior did and does, to become filled with charity. "Feast upon the words of Christ, for behold, the words of Christ will tell you all things what ye should do." (2 Nephi 32:3.)

We could love more if we sinned less, because studies have shown that sin runs down our batteries. Many things are a drain on our batteries, things such as hate, contention, envy, anger. Maybe love takes some changing. Some repenting. Turning.

Many of us want to serve, but suffer from "serv-o-phobia" — a fear of serving. We wonder what people will think, or say. Many times it takes courage to respond to promptings from the Spirit. We may find ourselves doing and saying things which surprise others *and* us. How come we're not kinder? It's so easy to do once we get going, and the world needs it so.

We'll have more time to love and enjoy helping if we're not hooked on things that waste our time or strength or keep our heart and mind unwisely occupied. Television, books, magazines, spending money, or whatever. Let's spend less time, energy, and money on things we don't really need. Our love for God and each other can deepen and sweeten as we *expect* less and *appreciate* more. Become more *grateful*. Simplify.

In our world, our society, our culture, let's not make spontaneous acts of love and charity and kindness and genuine compassion the "unusual thing." As my friend George Durrant says: "When it comes to giving, some people stop at nothing." Don't *ever* ignore an impulse to

46

serve *when there's something you could do*. It's important to recognize when you *can't* as well as when you *can*. Don't *ever* withhold love from someone *when it's within your power to give it*. If we could really figure out how to love, how to exercise charity, we wouldn't need a whole lot of other commandments.

It's destructive if we *feel* (charity, compassion, empathy) without *doing* something (when we're able). We diminish our power to act, to respond (like the "disuse phenomena," which teaches: That which we do not utilize diminishes in size and usefulness). When we withhold love we make it less possible for the Savior to reach out. Sometimes I act as if Christ had never come — had not lived, had not suffered, had not died, had not come again, had not loved *us* and forgiven *us* and been merciful, as if He had never asked us to love one another as He has loved us, as He does love us. We need to seek to become consistently Christlike. We eventually, finally, turn into that which we most desire to be, and we use our time and our life and all our other resources for that which we really desire to do and become.

As we become more Christlike, we can be called on to help because *we'll be there!* And it will be a sweet feeling to know that they knew it — they knew *you'd* stop and help. And we don't need to worry that we'll run out of places for our love and people who need it if we all start loving more. There are and will always be plenty of ways to share love and plenty of people who need it.

In John 13:35 we are taught, "By this shall all men

know that ye are my disciples, if ye have love one to another." It's how we treat each other and feel about each other. Jesus really *does* want me, and you, for a Sunbeam! The developing and exercising of charity is a way to show the meaning and value and result of the gospel in our lives. Love allowed the Atonement and all that was and is part of it.

Love is a *tenderizer*. It softens hearts. Love is the most basic of all human needs. To be hungry for love is a terrible kind of hunger. To be without comfort and attention is a terrible kind of nakedness. To yearn for companionship and to be needed is a terrible thirst. It's not only your words, your clothing, your food, your loaf of bread—it's *you!* God is love, and *you* are love! Teach me all that I must know . . . do . . . *be* . . . to live with Him *comfortably* some day. Who we are is more important than what we do, but who we are causes us to do what we do.

We work to be *fit* for the kingdom—not just worthy, but *comfortable. Fit!* To go to heaven—to belong there—we must take it with us. What are the criteria the Savior lists which will qualify us to hear Him say, "Come unto me, ye blessed"? If you still have your CTR ring? If you've used a dozen colors to mark your scriptures? Whether you can quote from *Johnny Lingo?* If you've memorized your "Tropical" Guide? If your great-great grandparents came across the plains? If you have five hundred pounds of wheat stored somewhere?

No. He will say, "Come unto me, ye blessed. I was

48

hungry, thirsty. You gave me shelter, refuge, time and attention, gentleness, mercy, and forgiveness." A cup of cold water in the name of Jesus Christ. Charity never faileth, and charity is a drink for someone who's thirsty. Some have been hungry and thirsty for such a long, long time. He wants us to live together in love and unity (see Mosiah 18:21). As Leo Tolstoy has said:

> I knew before that God gives life to men, and desires them to live; but now I know far more. I know that God does not desire men to live apart from each other, and therefore has not revealed to them what is needful for each of them to live by himself. He wishes them to live together, **united,** and therefore has revealed to them that they are needful to each other's happiness. I know now that people only **seem** to live when they care only for themselves, and that it is by love for others that they really live. He who has love has God in him, and is in God — because God is love.

The perfecting of the saints is plural and not just singular. Maybe it's our whole society, so that we may be *Zion* again. Pure in heart. *Pure* heart — what does it mean? A *change* of heart — a *new* heart. No hard-heartedness. One heart, one mind. Doing our best to live the gospel. No poor among us. Anywhere in the world? Are people in Brazil and Romania and New York and the Philippines and Kenya part of *us?* Yes. And we are part of them.

In some situations, a loaf of bread is more of a luxury

than gold. A glass of water is as valuable as a diamond if you're thirsty enough. What if we concentrated on just one thing and, for example, were more careful with water? Avoiding waste. Low-tech love again. Could we share some with those in the world who are thirsty? There are so many little things, like not leaving the water running when we don't need it. Many of us are probably hungry, lonely, thirsty, tired—or have been. If we knew the *heavy* burdens of those around us, it would make our hearts ache forever.

Charity will qualify us to be with our Heavenly Family once again. Love is worth it—it's worth giving our time and our life to. Could *He* have done more? Have I done all I could? Have *we?* If we fill our heart, our life, our home, our neighborhood, our community, and our whole world with love, then there's no room for hate, contention, anger, impatience, envy, unkindness, and other things which make us sick and sad and are such a drain on our batteries. And if you give love and serve one who does not seem to deserve it, God will not be mad at you. Let Him be the Judge . . . just love *everyone!*

I have come to know that the gospel of Jesus Christ is full of beautiful words, all related to the word *charity.* Words such as *feed, hug, mourn, serve, forgive, lift, succor, comfort, share, visit.* Love is what makes us *whole.* Love perfects us. If we really have charity, with all that it means, then peace happens, and *Zion can* be a reality. Let love and service with compassion become your need, your want, and your source of joy.

50

In this world there is enough loneliness and sorrow. There are enough people who are overwhelmed and discouraged. There are plenty of burdens and tears and unanswered *whys*. But in this world there is quite enough love for all of us and for all the world. And there is quite enough joy for all the world. Plenty of laughter and optimism and hugs. And there's enough hope and enough power to chase away any gloom. Because Jesus Christ is the Savior and Redeemer of the world, and the Atonement is a reality, and we can be with Him and our Father again.

May *we* "clap our hands" and exclaim the desires of our hearts to lift others' heavy burdens that they may be light, and bearable — that we are willing to mourn with those that mourn, and comfort those that stand in need of comfort. We will seek and find them. We will stop to help. We will lift hearts, strengthen feeble knees, comfort and bless and smile and give love. He loves us. He will help us. He understands when we can't do what we wish we could. God can heal all our wounds and help us with all our struggling. God the Father and His Son Jesus Christ can say: "I know just how you feel."

May God bless us with His Spirit and with the *gift* of charity, that it may be well with us when we see Him again. Charity never fails. And the more I learn about it, the more I feel to shout once more, "No wonder!" It never fails to move one soul to reach out to another. And it never fails to come back and comfort and bless the one who has given and given. It never fails to give us the assurance that God lives and Christ is our Savior.

51

Strengthen Families

by Anne C. Pingree

In Singapore there is a gentle custom. When a young woman leaves her parents' home to establish a home of her own, she presents her mother with a basket of gifts which represent all the things her mother has taught her. These gifts, which are well thought out and carefully made, include food delicacies, handwork, paintings, or writings as well as gifts symbolic of qualities such as patience and cheerfulness. They include souvenirs from happy family or personal experiences. In retrospect, a young woman realizes that *she* is the product of her own home and of the people with whom she shares it. In anticipation, she prepares herself to pass these gifts on to others.

All Families Are Important

Passing our knowledge, skills, and faith on to others is a big part of what families are all about. It is in anti-

cipation of what our families will become that we press
forward day after day, teaching and strengthening one
another. "The founding of the home is as sacred a work
as the founding of a church." (David O. McKay, *Church
News,* October 11, 1958.) It is in the family unit that
we learn the most important lessons in life. Families are
put together in many different ways. Perhaps our family
consists of a mother, father, and children. It may be a
family made up of a single mother, a widow, a single
woman, or a single father. We may be part of a combined
family or a nuclear family. Each family unit is unique but
very important. Without question, "the family is a major
anchor for us all, whether or not we live close to our
immediate family or whether or not our families are all
members of the Church." ("The Mission of Relief Society," *Ensign,* January 1991, p. 74.)

In *every* family *great* things are possible. Relationships
in the home, interaction one with another, and a feeling
of being united and bonded together are all necessary to
strengthen families, no matter what the makeup. As
stated in one broadcast of "The Spoken Word," "When
a family functions well, it can be a neverending source
of love, strength and growth for its members." ("Family
Relationships," 3 March 1991.) It is within the family
that we teach and practice eternal concepts. "It is in the
home where . . . values are usually acquired, traditions
are fostered, and commitments to others are established."
(James E. Faust, *Ensign,* May 1987, pp. 80–81.)

"Home is a place for all that is good and enlightening

and true," said Chieko N. Okazaki, first counselor in the Relief Society General Presidency. (*Ensign*, January 1991, p. 74.) Strong families are the foundation of all great civilizations. We know that undeviating love and fidelity, internal harmony, honesty, cooperation, and living the Golden Rule are critical to the well-being of the family. A strong family needs a firm religious foundation with an underlying belief in God. In every way the family should be the great "workshop of the Lord" where we work together and where we try day after day to teach each other "to love one another and to serve one another" (Mosiah 4:15), and where we practice what we learn in order to become better disciples of our Savior.

We also teach what we are and what is important to us in our families. Every family unit has conscious or unconscious priorities which are somewhat like a mission statement that motivates us and reinforces our values. Some families place high priorities on excellence in studies while others stress the importance of excelling in music, art, or athletics. One family's focus was on the counsel contained in Mosiah 4:14: "And ye will not suffer your children that they go hungry, or naked; neither will ye suffer that they transgress the laws of God, and fight and quarrel one with another." This family valued peace and harmony in their home. Each time the mother observed her children quarreling, she would simply say, "Mosiah 4:14!" The children would stop bickering and remember their resolve to have a harmonious family. Eventually, the children reached the point where they themselves reminded one another of their goal in Mosiah 4:14.

Your family matters. That is true whether you live in North Carolina, in Mexico, in Japan, or in South Africa. Families are basically the same worldwide. They may do things a little differently. They may toss the dishwater out the window instead of draining it from the sink. Some mothers may push a stroller while others may carry their babies on their backs. But goals for their families are the same. They all want to defend, protect, and enhance the family. They all desire to enrich the quality of life of their family members, and they all have love and a strong commitment to their families. While it is true that others can support, the family is still the essential team needed to build successful relationships and strong, well-adjusted individuals.

The greatest forces in the world are being used against families and traditional family values. These values are being undermined in subtle and in not-so-subtle ways. Because of this assault on family values, it takes all of your best efforts to fortify your family. It takes hard work and planning. It takes sacrifice. "In the setting of the family . . . may I suggest that we give more of ourselves, that we give more good experiences that are love-producing and family-solidifying. Whether the times we give are measured in minutes or hours is not as important as what we do in them. It may be five minutes at a child's bedside each night or a fifteen-minute walk in the evening. It may be a day in the hills or a three-minute phone call from the office at midday. It may be a clever note to a little girl or a night out with a boy. It can even be the experience of a family home evening. It can even be the experience of a family learning to pray together and reading the scriptures and fasting together." (H. Burke Peterson, *Ensign,* January 1973, p. 115.) Whatever it takes, we must be willing to work hard and organize ourselves in order to preserve our families.

Organize to Build Strong Families

"Organize yourselves; prepare every needful thing; and establish a house, even a house of prayer, a house of fasting, a house of faith, a house of learning, a house of glory, a house of order, a house of God." (D&C 88:119.) Organization, commitment, and a dash of creativity all combine to make families work. Some families use creativity in connection with family home evening experiences which teach strong and abiding principles.

One family held a "home teacher appreciation night" to honor one of their home teachers on his recent mission call. The children wanted to be involved in supporting missionary work, so they started saving their earnings in preparation for the special night. One saved money from babysitting jobs; another saved money from a paper route. The younger children earned money doing household tasks. One week before the missionary was to enter the MTC, the families met together. They talked about the exciting preparations that precede a mission and, after a simple skit and song, the two families knelt together in prayer. Then the children presented a small but heavy package to the recently called missionary with instructions not to open it until he got home. To his surprise, he saw that the box contained separate notes and envelopes. It was apparent that there was money in the envelopes — pennies, nickels, and dimes. What an effective way this was to teach younger children about the joys of giving and looking forward to serving missions!

A widow organized a family home evening for her children and grandchildren on their grandfather's birthday. Through special games and activities they learned about their grandfather — his background, his education, his personality. They saw photographs of him at different stages of his life, and they heard how he and grandmother met. Lastly, they read from his journal and heard his strong testimony of Jesus Christ. His favorite foods were served for refreshments.

Comparative shopping was the focus of a busy working mother who needed to teach her children how to help. Leaving the home for the activity, they drove to the local supermarket where they had a "hands-on" experience buying the week's groceries while using the principles of comparison shopping learned the week before.

In addition to hard work, planning, and creative family home evenings, family councils can be an effective way to strengthen families. "The Family Council is one of the most important means of dealing with troublesome problems in a democratic manner. It is just what its name implies — a meeting of all members of the family in which problems are discussed and solutions sought. Each family can work out the details of the Family Council to suit its own needs; but the basic principles remain the same. Each member has the right to bring up a problem. Each one has the right to be heard. Together, all seek for a solution to the problem, and the majority opinion is upheld." (Rudolf Dreikurs and Vicki Soltz, *Children: The Challenge,* Meredith Press, 1964, pp. 301–5.)

To end the council on a positive note a mother in one family, acting as the heart of the home, reads messages of praise to each family member. These "love notes" have been written during the week, put in the love box, and opened at the conclusion of family council. Praise is given for extra effort and performance given in any endeavor. This note could focus on an admirable personal quality instead of an accomplishment. Other members of the family can also write "love notes" and put them in the "love box" to be read, but mother *always* does. Thus, family council becomes a reporting, goal-setting, problem-solving, and praising time for families.

Traditions strengthen families. The word *remember* is used countless times in the Book of Mormon as a means of tying one group of people to another. The same thing holds true in families. Traditions solidify individuals and cause them to "remember" the important principles they have been taught through their lives. Holidays are often times when traditions are established. One family repeats a special tradition each Thanksgiving. In an effort to teach gratitude and appreciation, each member writes an anonymous note of appreciation to a person who has influenced his life in a significant way. One year a child chose to write to a teacher at school; another wrote to a community leader. Other recipients of letters of appreciation from this family included friends, a Church leader, and a grandparent.

On Thanksgiving another extended family holds a devotional just after dinner to express tender feelings of gratitude and appreciation. It takes several hours to hear from all the members, but this tradition bonds the family even though great geographical distances prevent them from being together often.

Familyhood

Traditions, family councils, and family home evenings help develop "familyhood," a process of bringing the family together through planned activities and goals. A divorced mother with three daughters found that her priorities changed when her husband left. Instead of worrying about a clean house, she focused on the importance of bonding the family in meaningful ways. They worked together to maintain their yard in the summer; they learned to fix things around the house. In fact, one of the daughters became very good at repairs and is the one who now really enjoys fixing the sprinkling system.

"When a person you depend on is gone, you pick up and do things; you carry on together," said Kathryn, a divorced mother who teaches school. "You keep up your testimony and stay busy so you don't feel sorry for yourself, and you work hard to build a strong family." Kathryn and her family spend Sundays with her parents where her daughters enjoy discussing gospel principles with their grandparents. They have family prayer together, and they also play games together. Even though Kathryn worries about finances, broken cars, daily lesson plans for school, and preparation of Sunday lessons for Young Women, she takes the time to have family prayers before dinner on many evenings. She and her daughters plan picnics, go to parades, visit the mountains, and sit together each evening doing school work. Even though their challenges are great, this family is strong because they work together and play together. They experience a sense of "family-hood" as they deal with life on a day-to-day basis.

Ruth, a widow in her eighties, was living in Hawaii when her husband died. She taught school for ten years after his death until her five unmarried children were on their own. Now she strengthens her family through letters and frequent phone calls. Her home is a gathering place for five grandchildren who attend college forty miles away. They enjoy coming there on weekends to watch football games and stay with their grandmother. Ruth has a strong conviction that each individual is responsible for her own life regardless of what challenges she may face. She says, "I strengthen my family by being busy. My children are not responsible for my happiness."

She, however, is a strong catalyst in her family for supporting and strengthening her sons, daughters, and grandchildren. Every Monday morning Ruth picks her son up from the airport when he flies into the city for work. She is lovingly known as his "taxi." Besides picking him up, she goes with her son to his seminars. Even though she has heard his presentation many times, she loves to see the audience's reaction to his lectures, and her son enjoys having his mother with him. It makes him feel good. The feeling of "familyhood" is still strong in this large family comprised of more than thirty-four members because of Ruth's strong, ongoing influence and involvement.

Learn then Teach

"Good family life is the ultimate joy of our existence," and building strong, self-reliant family members is critical to the success of a family. (See "Family Relationships," 3 March 1991.) As we learn and then teach each other in our families, we have opportunities to reach out to strengthen those around us. Our influence can have a rippling effect like a pebble tossed into a calm pool of water. We can influence and strengthen others if we have been taught well in our families. We can reach out and exercise the true spirit of charity we have learned in our homes. Then every man is like our brother; every woman is our sister. "Think of your brethren [and sisters] like unto yourselves, and be familiar with all and free with your substance, that they may be rich like unto you," we are counseled by the prophet, Jacob, in the Book of Mormon. (Jacob 2:17.)

Jacob's counsel was taken to heart by Dalene, a thirty-four-year-old single woman from Indiana who was taught "by precept, example, and direct participation" the Relief Society motto, "Charity Never Faileth." "I watched my mother and father do visiting teaching and home teaching, bake and take food to those in need, visit the sick, give blessings, and take time out of busy schedules to listen, talk, or be there for someone in need." After graduation from nursing school and working for a year, Dalene felt a strong desire to serve a mission. She was called as a welfare services missionary to Chile where the principles she had been taught in her home blessed and strengthened the lives of many.

Among those whose lives were touched by the principles of love and charity Dalene learned in her family was Sister Sepulveda, a sixty-year-old convert to the Church of less than three years. "She was illiterate yet she loved the gospel. The Book of Mormon was one of her greatest treasures, and her greatest desire in life was to be able to read it. Sister Sepulveda traveled six miles by bus each week to Church when she had the money. Otherwise, she walked the distance with her granddaughter in spite of heat, rain, or snow," Dalene said.

For eight months, Dalene spent forty-five minutes three times a week teaching Sister Sepulveda how to recognize the alphabet, how to pronounce vowels and consonants, and how to recognize simple words. "It seemed to me as time was passing, that she would never learn, and that this was a futile effort.

"On one of the rainiest days of the year, Sister Sepulveda arrived one hour late for the lesson at the chapel. My companion and I were just preparing to leave when she came in the chapel doors. She was soaked from head to toe, and she had on an old wool coat that had no buttons. She held it tightly closed in front of her as she hobbled along. Her hair was long and grey, and it was matted to her head. She looked like a drowned rat. Her feet and ankles were swollen. I told her she shouldn't have come, and her response was, 'Oh, Hermana, I promised the Lord if he'd just send me someone to teach me to read, I would never miss a lesson or Church meeting!'

"I worked with Sister Sepulveda to the end of my mission. As I was preparing to leave and saying good-byes to all who had so richly blessed my life, Sister Sepulveda gave me a letter she had written in her *own* hand. She told me that as we had learned letters, she began practicing to trace them and copy them at night. She worked by a kerosene lamp with her bad eyes. Her fingers and hands were swollen with arthritic joints, yet she practiced the letters with her granddaughter's help. This was *her* gift to me."

A young black single mother and her family struggling to make ends meet in the ghettos of Chicago, Illinois, is strengthened through homemaking meetings carefully planned to meet the needs of the 202 sisters in the Hyde Park Ward. Sister Hattie Soil, a wise and farsighted Relief Society president, has a desire to use the Relief Society program to teach eighty black sisters. Many are single and divorced parents needing to break the cycle of four generations of welfare and to learn to survive on incomes far below poverty level. Homemaking meetings are organized to help these women learn principles of budgeting, effective childcare, basic sewing, home organization, and canning fruits and vegetables.

When a twenty-two-year-old single mother of three children ages five, three, and one joined the Church, she knew very little about caring for her children and was living in a very dangerous situation. Her rat-infested apartment had a hole in the floor which dropped clear to the basement and was hazardous for her crawling baby. She came to feel the great influence of Sister Soil's vision of how Relief Society could be used to strengthen her home and young family. Sister Soil and the ward bishop visited the young mother and subsequently helped her move out of the bad housing and into a cleaner apartment located in a rehabilitated building nearby which rented for the same price.

In homemaking meeting this same single mother is learning to break the cycle of welfare which has been a part of her background for four generations. Her children are now safe, clean, and well cared for, and she is learning how to budget her $400 monthly income check as well as how to can fruits and vegetables. She is putting aside a portion of her canned goods for food storage and has learned creative ways to store them, including under her bed. In addition to learning these important skills, this young mother is enrolled in a Church literacy program where she is learning to read. Her goal is to acquire a high school diploma, learn typing skills, and reach a point where she can get a job and grow in independence and self-confidence.

Individual women can richly bless the lives of others when they put into practice the principles they have learned in Relief Society. A strong gospel foundation gleaned from years of spiritual living as well as home and family education lessons may have helped two sisters touch the life of a nonmember woman living in their neighborhood. They acted on the counsel of President Spencer W. Kimball who declared in a Churchwide women's conference in September 1979: "I stress again the deep need each woman has to study the scriptures. Become scholars of the scriptures," he said, "not to put others down but to lift them up." ("The Role of Righteous Women," *Ensign*, November 1979, pp. 102–4.) He told women that as they become more and more familiar with the truths of the scriptures, they will not only bless their own families, but will become more effective in keeping the second great commandment of loving their neighbors as themselves.

That opportunity to lift and love a neighbor came to a pair of sisters. Their bishop, through the Relief Society president, asked them to visit and become a friend to Linda, a Catholic neighbor living in their area. Linda was experiencing challenges in her marriage as well as with her children. She opened her door to these new friends who began to visit her on a regular basis. For only a few short months they took kind and understanding hearts and their love of the gospel into Linda's home. Hearing her problems, they shared their insight and experience. Linda listened and asked questions. She spoke openly of her beliefs and concerns. And then one wintry day in December she announced to her friends that she and her family would be moving across the country in one week to Florida where her husband had a job opportunity.

Linda's new friends wanted to give her a Christmas gift before she left, but they weren't sure what it should be. Finally, after much thought and prayer, they bought a copy of the Book of Mormon and had Linda's name imprinted on the front of it. Inside the cover they slipped letters in which they shared their testimonies of the truthfulness of the Book of Mormon and the joy and peace the gospel of Jesus Christ had brought to them and their families. Then they wrapped their special Christmas gift and presented it to Linda a few days before she moved.

The weeks and months passed with no word from Linda. Her Relief Society friends wondered if they had offended her with their testimonies of Jesus Christ and their gift. Then one day—two years later—a letter came from Florida. In it Linda told how she had read the Book of Mormon while making that long, cross-country trip. She wrote how she had eventually asked for the missionaries to come and teach her, and she described how she had joined the Church and been sealed to her family in the Atlanta Temple.

Because two women shared what they had been

taught, the Book of Mormon became a moving force in Linda's life, and she said in a letter to them: "You will never know how I hold this gift of the Book of Mormon so dear to me. Your Christmas gift changed my life so much. I carry your gift with me to all my Church meetings. I read my scriptures daily, and your gift to me is more than a part of life—it is my life."

What an influence committed women of these latter days can have in their homes and in their neighborhoods! In spite of challenges, difficulties, and less-than-perfect families, all of us can work toward building *righteous* families. We can also reach outside our families to strengthen those around us. The gift of knowledge, understanding, and testimony remains an empty gift unless we use it to bless the lives of our families and those around us.

"To teach, you must first learn. To give, you must have something to offer. A woman who nurtures her spirit and mind, who expands her understanding and capacities, will have a rich harvest with which to feed others." (*Learn Then Teach*, The Church of Jesus Christ of Latter-day Saints.) As the gentle custom in Singapore suggests, a woman's basket of gifts gleaned from experiences and gospel concepts learned in her home and in Relief Society will be full and ready to share with others. "One woman's spirit and mind can bless thousands of lives." Her influence can be felt not only in her immediate family and in her neighborhood, but also through generations to come.

Enjoy a Unified Sisterhood

by Carol L. Clark

I felt awful. It was the week after Thanksgiving, I had just broken up with my boyfriend, I was thirty-five and childless, and I was living alone and feeling very sorry for myself. I ran into a wonderful friend, a woman older than I—also single—who I felt sure could comfort and counsel me. Over dinner at her house, I poured out my frustrations, my anger, my loneliness.

Without sympathy or hesitation she responded, "Carol, if you don't have a family, make one."

"Make one!" In a big dose of spiritual reality therapy, Elizabeth wisely reminded me that I can create—and enjoy—something quite wonderful myself, a bounteous series of relationships with the Lord and with his children, who are my brothers and sisters.

The fifth part of the Relief Society mission statement encourages us to "enjoy a unified sisterhood." This suggestion that we make a family of each other seems fitting to me as the conclusion of our mission. We LDS women, like the people instructed by King Benjamin, "believe in Jesus Christ, the Son of God, who created heaven and earth, and all things." (Mosiah 4:2.) I believe that like these people we can be "filled with joy, having received a remission of [our] sins, and having peace of conscience, because of the exceeding faith which [we have] in Jesus Christ." (Mosiah 4:3.)

I also believe we can be "filled with joy" as we make of one another a family of daughters of God and sisters in Zion who share faith in Jesus Christ.

Make a Family

The scriptures live for me — in technicolor with dolby sound. When I encounter these people of other times and places, I am counseled by their lives and teachings.

One story I particularly enjoy is that of Alma the Elder. Here was a man of high political and religious standing who was converted by hearing instructions from a prophet of God to an evil king. Alma taught others and they joined him at "a place which was called Mormon." (Mosiah 18:4) From him they learned about making a family in the truest sense: "And he commanded them that there should be no contention one with another but that they should look forward with one eye, having one faith and one baptism, having their hearts knit together in unity and in love one towards another." (Mosiah 18:21.)

With "*one* eye, *one* faith, *one* baptism," they dealt

with *one* another in unity and love. What a remarkable thing to be "knit together in unity and love" with the family of Saints.

I presume that Alma and his people succeeded in their "knitting," for their story continued, "and thus they became the children of God." (Mosiah 18:22.) How did they do it? How can we do it?

Clearly, we must want to do it. We start by recognizing that being a literal daughter of God is not enough. We must also become the spiritual children of God, something that does not occur, as Alma's people experienced, until we bond together. This bonding is more than sitting or talking or listening or singing together. To become the children of God, we must be knit together. This bonding means believing, covenanting, and working together in loving unity. The bonding that makes us the children of God also truly makes a family of us.

Learning that King Noah "sent his army to destroy them" (Mosiah 18:33), Alma and his people "departed into the wilderness" (Mosiah 18:34). This band of people left behind their indoor plumbing and refrigerators, their social groups and their professions. Maybe some of them came with their entire family units, maybe some of them came alone, maybe some of them came without daughters or fathers. We cannot say. All we know is that something wonderful happened among these people who learned what it is to make family of one another.

In Relief Society we talk about sisterhood a lot. We designate each other as sisters, we call Relief Society our ward sisterhood, we comment about our worldwide sisterhood. What we're really talking about is making a family.

I take this business of family relationships very seriously. Perhaps this is because, as a single woman without children, I know what it is like not to have a family. Hence, when we Relief Society women call each other "sister," I think quite literally of this as a title that means we are family—we are connected in a unique, lasting, personal way. And when these connections are not just taped or spliced or lashed together but rather knit together, wonderful things happen.

Affection

My friend Blythe (aptly named) is an orphan. Her parents died when she was a teenager, and her brother, not a member of the Church, has always lived far away. Some people might wither in such a circumstance.

Not Blythe. She is a thriving survivor, who also turns a fine phrase.

It is from her I learned the great line, "family by affection." She acknowledges that none of us can alter our blood family relationships. We are born into our families by blood. But because of the agency Heavenly Father has given us, we can choose our family by affection.

Just think of it—we can feel related to the people we love. And this means we can choose to make our family by blood also our family by affection. We can "adopt" and enfold them through the love we feel for them. Maybe this is what Paul was talking about when he said, "For ye have not received the spirit of bondage again to fear; but ye have received the Spirit of adoption, whereby we cry, Abba, Father. The Spirit itself beareth witness with our spirit, that we are the children of God: And if children, then heirs." (Romans 8:15–17.)

So we, children and heirs of God, can create large, warm families by affection. I think of this idea each time I sing "I Am a Child of God." If I am a child of God and you are a child of God, then we're sisters, right? And if we're sisters, let's love each other, adopt each other into a family by affection. In our family by affection we can enjoy close, warm, personal, meaningful relationships, whether or not we have them in our family by blood.

Allison, my niece by blood and affection, taught me what they say to each other in her family as they go off for the day. She never leaves home that she doesn't say to her mother, "Love you" instead of "Good-bye." Wouldn't it be nice if as we left Relief Society, we all said, "Love you" instead of "Have a good week"? Time, circumstances, and many pressures can steal our opportunities to feel bonded and one with our Relief Society sisters. Still, despite all the pulls of life, whenever we join together, I seek opportunities to enfold my Relief Society family in my arms as I enfold them in my heart.

Parents, children, siblings, even spouses may leave us. We may never have loving family by blood. Yet through the gospel, we can be family. Neither you nor

I need ever feel orphaned anymore than my blithe-spirited friend does.

Humor

When I've shared a good laugh with a woman, I consider her my sister and buddy. *Buddy* is a word with warmth for me because of a ward Relief Society president who singlehandedly made me feel welcome in a ward of seven hundred.

I had just bought my first home and was finding the transition to homeowner to be a bit taxing. I was trying to paint, unbox my life, carry the demanding load at work, and feel at home with it all. During those first weeks as I sat alone in a huge congregation at sacrament meeting, I felt very disaffiliated. It seemed that the new couples had each other, the established couples had each other and I had little way of introducing myself into this massive group of groups.

Then MarJean found me. MarJean was the ward Relief Society president. Most of all she was a buddy. From the moment she introduced herself to me and me to others, MarJean watched out for me. Each week she would find me in the crowd and tell me some wonderful little story. Invariably at the end of it she would say, "Isn't that funny?" And it was. She talked about bouncing on the new mattress, about going to her son's rugby game, about hugging a wet baby, about exploring the thrift stores. It was all engaging and funny.

Soon I looked forward to those weekly visits and was

delighted to discover that MarJean hung around the local grocery at 10:30 P.M. too. We'd run into each other in the frozen foods and talk and chuckle our way from the petite peas to the ice cream bars.

As I met her family and came to love them, I was drawn into their world. Over her husband, Blaine's, celestial waffles, her children and various family by affection, like me, would talk about the world and the weirdness and wonders of life. And often we had cause for a good laugh.

MarJean helped me enjoy my transition into the ward. With her at the helm, Relief Society was like a party to which all were cordially invited. I always sensed that MarJean had laughed with each of them as she laughed with me. The result: we felt at ease with each other. We felt close to each other. We were buddies.

I learned from MarJean that if I don't spend some time enjoying a good laugh with a buddy everyday, I am missing some of the great pleasures of life. Nothing is more bonding than a good laugh or a good cry, and humor gives us an excuse for both.

I weathered another broken romance, increasing job demands, my first winter of snow shoveling, a torn up basement, and much more during my sojourn in that ward. And I weathered it much better because MarJean had taught me to say, "Isn't that funny?" even when it was awful.

Diversity

My friend Suzanne and I don't have a thing in common. We do not belong to the same church. We do not have many of the same values. We do not look at the world in the same way. Yet, she's the one I get my opera tickets with because Suzanne is a trusted, tried friend. What bonds us?

I think it's primarily our diversity. Each of us enjoys learning how the other thinks and why. We have a great time laughing, talking, sharing together. I always like the opera, but I always love talking to Suzanne.

I thank the Lord daily that I am alive in a time of great diversity. I love the changes in the world, in the Church. Perhaps this is because I don't find changing particularly easy to do in my own life, so I love the constant challenge of having to do it and of learning from others how to do it. I love the personal challenge and reward of being part of a worldwide Church, a worldwide sisterhood.

I am blessed to serve in Relief Society now. I serve with fine, committed women, many of whom are not like me. We have not had the same life experiences, we do not view the world the same, we do not think alike. All of this is wonderful to me. It means that whenever we gather, I enjoy fresh ideas, new thoughts, great scriptural insights, and broadened vistas about everything in the world.

In my Relief Society sisterhood, we are not alike. Yet we are one as we are unified in purpose and direction.

This unity is something we have discussed and about which we often pray, for we know that through unified diversity we are all bettered. We are not all alike. What a blessing!

In my salad days in Relief Society, years ago, I was intimidated by the knowledge others had that I didn't possess. A memorable case in point was my first committee assignment when I began my serious involvement in Relief Society at age twenty-five. I didn't know anyone. I thought I had little to offer. I felt terribly insecure.

This first assignment was to serve on the Christmas party committee. We held our first meeting in the elegant home of an elegant hostess, our committee chair. We sat around her kitchen table, and I immediately noticed she had a built-in marble slab in her counter. I was terribly impressed, as a built-in marble slab for making candy symbolized to me the ultimate in kitchens, the ultimate in homemaking.

I gasped when the committee chair asked me to bring caramels to the party—by-me-made caramels. I glanced at the marble slab in horror. I had never made candy in my life. I didn't have a clue how a body even made caramels.

After the meeting ended, I headed for the home of a good friend. I told Meredith and her mother about my caramel assignment. I said that maybe I should just ask to be released because not only was I a candy illiterate, I was also a sewing illiterate. The Relief Society was sure to discover these voids soon enough, so it might be better if I confessed all so they could just release me and get it over with.

Pat, Meredith's mother, advised prudence. My own mother and sister, she reminded me, made wonderful candy. They would certainly help me. I shouldn't panic. My reputation was not on the line. My life was not ending. These were only caramels, after all. Meredith added that the candy everyone made would be put together on platters. No one would know which I'd made anyway, so what was I worried about.

But I was worried. I made the caramels — all alone — with my mother standing on my left hand and my sister standing on my right. At my request, they monitored every beat of the spoon.

What I learned later was that few of those Relief Society women had marble slabs in their kitchens. Some of them didn't even like candy. My own green expectations created the stress I felt.

The truth was that they were diverse in many ways. In time, I quit worrying about caramels and started learning from this treasure of women, many of whom shaped the opinions and working styles I have leaned on heavily in subsequent years. Our differences blessed me by giving me various righteous role models from which I mined many skills. I formed friendships that have lasted nearly twenty years and have enriched my life beyond expression. Those caramels I painstakingly made were sweet; learning from my sisters has been far sweeter.

Fine Ideas

I have savored many a moment spent with a fine idea and a friend.

Recently I received a four-page, single-spaced letter of fine ideas from a brand new friend. I consider it a treasure. I consider it such because ideas shared from the heart are so rich, and Mary Ellen shared from her heart.

One idea Mary Ellen shared was about communication. She suggested that "maybe the pure in thought and heart had practiced the skill so much that they were able to perceive the thoughts and intents of others' hearts. Perhaps here lies a key to there being 'no poor among them.' The pure in heart and thought might know each other's strugglings and sorrow, each other's poverty, each other's spiritual, social, physical and other needs."

What a powerful idea, this concept of spiritual communication. I've thought about it, made it a consideration in my scripture study, in my prayers. It's something Mary Ellen and I can talk about for a long time to come. I am grateful for Mary Ellen, I am grateful for the idea.

Years ago I became conscious of D&C 43:8: "And now, behold, I give unto you a commandment, that when ye are assembled together ye shall instruct and edify each other, that ye may know how to act and direct my church, how to act upon the points of my law and commandments, which I have given."

This counsel to instruct and edify appeals greatly to me. At best our interaction with each other should do both—teach and lift. What's even better is to know that we *can* teach and lift each other.

I have some good friends I see about once a month. We gather for what we call "Friday Breakfast." On the first Friday of the month we congregate at a local restaurant early in the morning, head for a back table, and enjoy an hour's worth of chat. Sometimes it's rather mundane, sometimes it's heated, sometimes it's personal, sometimes it's professional. Always it's fun.

As part of our group's activity, we gather on an erstwhile basis for birthday parties. If your birthday is within two months either way, the party counts for you. Our parties are happy celebrations, full of cake, ice cream, and song. Last year at the party honoring me, among others, Jeanie, our hostess, asked each person to bring a favorite thought to share with the honorees.

After we sang every birthday song we knew—it turns out to be quite a few—Jeanie asked each woman to read her thought. Suddenly the party became a spiritual experience. As each of my sisters read her thought, I was edified and instructed. I learned something about each one. I was instructed by her comments on the thought she shared. I was edified by the spirit of the Lord each woman invited into our party. It was a celebration of the fine ideas the Lord had blessed each of us to understand and love.

Lots of times I sit in Relief Society and think about what each sister brings to the party. We sing songs together—we know quite a few—and we share ideas.

Whenever a sister of mine shares from her heart something she has learned, I am edified. I am grateful I'm in the company of women who hold fine ideas dear.

Spiritual Friendship

Two years ago, I took a business trip to Canada. My dad drove me to the airport, and as he closed the trunk of the car and turned to send me off, I gave him a hug and said, "Dad, I love you."

Those were the last words I ever spoke to my father. He died of a massive heart attack the next day.

As I struggled to get home through that endless night, I sat for six hours in the Calgary airport alone. What happened to me beginning there has changed me permanently.

I read Moses' words: "I call heaven and earth to record this day against you, that I have set before you life and death, blessing and cursing: therefore choose life, that both thou and thy seed may live; That thou mayest love the Lord thy God, and that thou mayest obey his voice, and that thou mayest cleave unto him; for he is thy life, and the length of thy days." (Deuteronomy 30:19–20.)

My beloved father had chosen life; he had chosen the Lord. As people spoke to members of my family during subsequent days, most spoke of a personal moment shared with dad as he had been a friend, a bishop, a business partner. No one ever mentioned business success or cars or nice homes.

What my father left them was also what he left us —

something permanent — for he left spiritually based friendships. I can say, "Dad, I love you," not just because he's my father, but also because with Norman Clark I share a spiritual friendship and a great deal of affection.

Sometimes I think about what makes Relief Society different from other women's groups. What can I get/give in Relief Society that I can't experience somewhere else? For me the answer always hinges on spiritual friendships. In Relief Society I join with a group of women who share my love of the Lord. Our friendships, our familial relationships are based upon that which endures, i.e., the gospel of Jesus Christ. Solid friendships I can find many places, but spiritually solid friendships I can have through the sisterhood of Relief Society. Like my father, I would "choose life" that I may grow in my capacity to create friendships that bind me spirit to spirit with other individuals. What other type of friendship can ever be as satisfying, comforting, or enduring?

Charity Never Faileth

There they were, the people of Alma the Elder. We do not know all they sacrificed, we do know it was at least their homes and most of their possessions.

What happened to them? Amulon, in cahoots with some Lamanites, captured them. Having also been a priest of King Noah, Amulon knew Alma and took perverse pleasure in tormenting these new converts to the Lord's church. "And it came to pass that so great were their afflictions that they began to cry mightily to God. And

Amulon commanded them that they should stop their cries; and he put guards over them to watch them, that whosoever should be found calling upon God should be put to death." (Mosiah 24:10–11.)

I have often wondered how I might have responded to this loss of connection with my fellow believers. Unable to worship or even pray with others, would I have been able to maintain faith?

Alma and his people seemed to grow their faith in such tough times. "And Alma and his people did not raise their voices to the Lord their God, but did pour out their hearts to him; and he did know the thoughts of their hearts. It came to pass that the voice of the Lord came to them in their afflictions, saying: Lift up your heads and be of good comfort, for I know the covenant which ye have made with me, and I will covenant with my people and deliver them out of bondage." (Mosiah 24:12–13.)

Two things strike me about these verses: first, the Lord spoke to each person individually; second, the Lord said the same thing to each person individually.

These people were together — literally and figuratively. Each was righteous enough to be prayerfully capable of receiving instruction from the Lord. Each was united enough with her brothers and sisters, and received the same message.

The Lord rescued the people of Alma the Elder from bondage. I am convinced this miraculous rescue was possible because these people loved and lived charity. "Charity never faileth" is the Relief Society motto; it is also a statement about how we can choose to treat each other. Alma's people "did walk uprightly before God, imparting to one another both temporally and spiritually according to their needs and their wants." (Mosiah 18:29.) I believe that once these people understood what it meant to "impart" to each other, they made a family by affection of each other. They created spiritual friendships that endured the most arduous trial. They were bonded through their living of the law of charity.

In Relief Society I see myself bonded—how different from being in bondage—with 2.8 million women worldwide. Often when I do my visiting teaching I think of the women who do their visiting teaching in Kansas or France or Guam. Sometimes I think of myself as ringing a doorbell at the very moment my sister in Canada is doing the same thing. In Relief Society I am part of something bigger than myself.

As a visiting teacher what I do is important because I exercise watchcare of another woman. What I do is also important in a global sense. I am one of thousands of women who are together—literally and figuratively. We do this work because we love the Lord and we feel a kinship with our sisters. Through our "imparting" one to another we learn of the Lord, we discover how to be like Him, we rejoice in each other. I am part of a righteous sisterhood building the kingdom of God throughout the earth. What my sisters and I do together and individually matters.

Together now and forever we enjoy our unified sisterhood.

Index

Accountability, 29

Affection, bonds of, 72–74

Agency, wise use of, 27–29

Alma the Elder, people of, 70–71, 82–84

Art, bearing witness through, 14–16

"At the Garden Tomb, John 1:5," poem, 15

Ball, Jeffrey, 14

Ball, Joyce, 14

Basket of gifts, Singapore tradition of, 53

Blind woman, observations of, 26–27

Boasting, 36–37

Bolivia, missionary killed in, 14

Book of Mormon, sisters share, with nonmember neighbor, 66–68

Bookstore, author buys, 22–23

Bowden, Elva, 11

Bowden, Marvin, 11

Bunting, Mary, 24

Burdens: gaining strength to bear, 23–24, 39; bearing one another's, 51

Caramels, homemade, 77–78

Charity: service implied in, 34; as motto and heart of Relief Society, 34–35; scriptural definition of, 36–39; unfailing nature of, 39–40; begins with willingness, 41–42; seeking promptings in, 42; and "low-tech" love, 42–43; and law of fast, 44–

45; acting on impulses in, 46–47; as key to eternal life, 48–49; gift of, 51. *See also* Compassionate service; Service

"Charity Never Faileth," 34–35, 39–40, 63

Chicago, Illinois, special homemaking meetings in, 64–65

Choices and consequences, 29

Church of Jesus Christ of Latter-day Saints: barring of, from Ghana, 7–8; diversity of members of, 17–18, 76; drawing of righteous women to, 28–29

Clark, Norman, 81–82

Communication, spiritual, 79

Compassionate service, 30–31; may involve sacrifice or inconvenience, 40–41; seeking promptings in, 42. *See also* Charity; Service

Construction project, testimony likened to, 1–2

Covenants, making, 12

Creativity, expressing, 24–26

Decisions, confirmation of, through prayer, 11–12

Discipleship: definition of, 6–7; role of love in, 47–48

Diversity: beauty in, 17–19; bonding through, 76–78

Divorced mother shares family ideas, 60–61

Dreikurs, Rudolf, 58–59

Dunn, Paul H., 9

Durrant, George, 46

Education, ongoing program of, 24–25

Eternal life, key to, is charity, 48–49

Exclusivity, charity prevents, 38

Faith: growing in, 2; and testimony, 3; nurturing, in others, 3–4

Families: lessons passed on in, 53–54; uniqueness of, 54; eternal concepts practiced in, 54–55; priorities of, 55; basic similarities of, 56; fortifying, against worldly assaults, 56–57; organization in, 57–59; strengthening, through traditions, 59–60; extending influence of, into world, 62; "making," of Lord's children, 69–70; "by affection," 72–74

Family council, 58–59

Family home evenings, 57–58

"Familyhood," 60–62

Fasting, 44–45

Father, example set by, 81–82

Faust, James E., 54

Forgiveness, 38–39

Index

Friendship, spiritually solid, 82

Gas, women get, for stranded mother, 33–34
Ghana, Church barred from, 7–8
Gifts, discovering individual, 19, 25
Guidance, accepting, from Lord, 22–23

Holmes, Oliver Wendell, 1
Homemaking, meetings geared to special needs, 64–66
Hope: association of, with future, 4–5; exhibited by pioneer foremothers, 5–6; of improving life's conditions, 6
Humor, building bonds through, 74–75

Ideas, sharing, with friends, 79–81
Individuals: inherent worth of, 17, 31; diversity of, 17–19; gifts of, 19, 25; personal missions of, 20–23; creative expression of, 24–26; obstacles overcome by, 26–27
Influence, exerting, for good, 27–28, 66, 68

Jack, Elaine L., 19
Jesus Christ: receiving personal witness of, 19–20; gives strength to bear burdens, 23–24; principles of charity taught by, 36–37; becoming like, 47

Kenya, interrogation of Church representatives in, 11
Kimball, Spencer W., 28–29, 66

Larsen, JoAnn, 25–26
Learn, then teach, 68
Love: following Christ's promptings in, 34; pure, implies service, 34; involves energy and work, 41; sin as roadblock to, 46; withholding, 47; disciples identified by, 47–48; as basic human need, 48; unconditional, 50. *See also* Charity
Love notes, 59
"Low-tech" love, 42–43

McKay, David O., 54
Missionary: family saves money to help, 57–58; teaches Chilean sister to read, 63–64
Mission statement of Relief Society, ix-x
Missions, personal, discovering and fulfilling, 20–23
Motto of Relief Society, 34–35

Obstacles, overcoming, 26–27
Okazaki, Chieko N., 54–55
Ordinances, participating in, 12–13
Organization in families, 57–59

Paths, analogy of, 20–22
Patience, 38
Patriarchal blessing, Hungarian woman receives, 5
Peterson, H. Burke, 56–57
Pioneer women, hope of, 5–6
Praise, 43–44
Prayer: as safeguard, 10; to bless others, 10–11; effective, 11–12; being an answer to someone's, 41
Priorities, family, 55

Relief Society: mission statement of, ix-x; as ongoing education program, 24–25; charity is at heart of, 34–35; sisterhood of, 71–72, 84–85; spiritually solid friendships built through, 82

Sacrament, covenants of, 12
Safeguard, prayer as, 10
Scriptures: gaining knowledge of, 8–10, 66; charity defined in, 36–39; as handbook of instructions for service, 45–46
Self-esteem, growing in, 25–26
Sepulveda, Sister, 63–64

Service: pure love implies, 34; instructions for, in scriptures, 45–46; fear of, 46; following impulses in, 46–47. *See also* Charity; Compassionate service
Singapore, gift-giving tradition in, 53
Single woman is counseled to "make a family," 69–70
Sisterhood of Relief Society, 71–72, 84–85
Soil, Hattie, 64–65
Soltz, Vicki, 58–59

Talents, sharing, 25
Testimony: as long-term construction project, 1–2; role of faith in, 2–4; role of hope in, 4–6; and thoughtful discipleship, 6–8; and knowledge of scriptures, 8–10; role of prayer in, 10–12; role of covenants and ordinances in, 12–13; and bearing witness, 13–16; individual, 19–20
Time, wise use of, 46
Tolstoy, Leo, 49
Traditions, strengthening families through, 59–60
Transitions, life, 29–30
Truth: finding, in scriptures, 9–10; rejoicing in, 39

Unity: in diversity, 18, 76–78;

of Zion, through love, 49; of
Alma's people, 70–71, 82–
84; of spiritual children of
God, 71

Visiting teaching, 84–85

"Wait a week," 43–44
Welfare, breaking cycle of
dependence on, 64–66
Willingness as beginning to
charity, 41–42

Witnesses of God: willingness
to stand as, 13–14; works of
art as, 14–16
Women, potential of, to
influence world for good, 28–
29, 66, 68

Young, Mary, 15

Zion, unity of, 49